Rosamund, Queen of the Lombards by Algernon Charles Swinburne

A TRAGEDY

Algernon Charles Swinburne was born on April 5th, 1837, in London, into a wealthy Northumbrian family. He was educated at Eton and at Balliol College, Oxford, but did not complete a degree.

In 1860 Swinburne published two verse dramas but achieved his first literary success in 1865 with Atalanta in Calydon, written in the form of classical Greek tragedy. The following year "Poems and Ballads" brought him instant notoriety. He was now identified with "indecent" themes and the precept of art for art's sake.

Although he produced much after this success in general his popularity and critical reputation declined. The most important qualities of Swinburne's work are an intense lyricism, his intricately extended and evocative imagery, metrical virtuosity, rich use of assonance and alliteration, and bold, complex rhythms.

Swinburne's physical appearance was small, frail, and plagued by several other oddities of physique and temperament. Throughout the 1860s and 1870s he drank excessively and was prone to accidents that often left him bruised, bloody, or unconscious. Until his forties he suffered intermittent physical collapses that necessitated removal to his parents' home while he recovered.

Throughout his career Swinburne also published literary criticism of great worth. His deep knowledge of world literatures contributed to a critical style rich in quotation, allusion, and comparison. He is particularly noted for discerning studies of Elizabethan dramatists and of many English and French poets and novelists. As well he was a noted essayist and wrote two novels.

In 1879, Swinburne's friend and literary agent, Theodore Watts-Dunton, intervened during a time when Swinburne was dangerously ill. Watts-Dunton isolated Swinburne at a suburban home in Putney and gradually weaned him from alcohol, former companions and many other habits as well.

Much of his poetry in this period may be inferior but some individual poems are exceptional; "By the North Sea," "Evening on the Broads," "A Nympholept," "The Lake of Gaube," and "Neap-Tide."

Swinburne lived another thirty years with Watts-Dunton. He denied Swinburne's friends access to him, controlled the poet's money, and restricted his activities. It is often quoted that 'he saved the man but killed the poet'.

Swinburne died on April 10th, 1909 at the age of seventy-two.

Index of Contents

PERSONS REPRESENTED
ALBOVINE, King of the Lombards.
ALMACHILDES, a young Lombard warrior.
NARSETES, an old leader and counsellor.
ROSAMUND, Queen of the Lombards
HILDEGARD, a noble Lombard maiden.

SCENE

Verona

TIME

June 573

ACT I

A hall in the Palace: a curtain drawn midway across it.

Enter **ALBOVINE** and **NARSETES**.

ALBOVINE
This is no matter of the wars: in war
Thy king, old friend, is less than king of thine,
And comrade less than follower. Hast thou loved
Ever—loved woman, not as chance may love,
But as thou hast loved thy sword or friend—or me?
Thou hast shewn me love more stout of heart than death.
Death quailed before thee when thou gav'st me life,
Borne down in battle.

NARSETES
Woman? As I love
Flowers in their season. A rose is but a rose.

ALBOVINE

Dost thou know rose from thistle or bindweed? Man,
Speak as our north wind speaks, if harsh and hard—
Truth.

NARSETES

White I know from red, and dark from bright,
And milk from blood in hawthorn-flowers: but not
Woman from woman.

ALBOVINE

How should God our Lord,
Except his eye see further than his world?
For women ever make themselves anew,
Meseems, to match and mock the maker. Friend,
If ever I were friend of thine in fight,
Speak, and I bid thee not speak truth: I know
Thy tongue knows nought but truth or silence.

NARSETES

Is it
A king's or friend's part, king, to bid his friend
Speak what he knows not? Speak then thou, that I
May find thy will and answer it.

ALBOVINE

I am fain
And loth to tell thee how it wrings my heart
That now this hard-eyed heavy southern sun
Hath wrought its will upon us all a year
And yet I know not if my wife be mine.

NARSETES

Thy meanest man at arms had known ere dawn
Blinked on his bridal birthday.

ALBOVINE

Did I bid thee
Mock, and forget me for thy friend—I say not,
King? Is thy heart so light and lean a thing,
So loose in faith and faint in love? I bade thee
Stand to me, help me, hold my hand in thine
And give my heart back answer. This it is,
Old friend and fool, that gnaws my life in twain—
The worm that writhes and feeds about my heart—
The devil and God are crying in either ear
One murderous word for ever, night and day,
Dark day and deadly night and deadly day,

Can she love thee who slewest her father? I
Love her.

NARSETES
Thy wife should love thee as thy sire's
Loved him. Thou art worth a woman—heart for heart.

ALBOVINE
My sire's wife loved him? Hers he had not slain.
Would God I might but die and burn in hell
And know my love had loved me!

NARSETES
Is thy name
Babe? Sweet are babes as flowers that wed the sun,
But man may be not born a babe again,
And less than man may woman. Rosamund
Stands radiant now in royal pride of place
As wife of thine and queen of Lombards—not
Cunimund's daughter. Hadst thou slain her sire
Shamefully, shame were thine to have sought her hand
And shame were hers to love thee: but he died
Manfully, by thy mightier hand than his
Manfully mastered. War, born blind as fire,
Fed not as fire upon her: many a maid
As royal dies disrobed of all but shame
And even to death burnt up for shame's sake: she
Lives, by thy grace, imperial.

ALBOVINE
He or I,
Her lord or sire, which hath most part in her,
This hour shall try between us.

[Enter **ROSAMUND**.

ROSAMUND
Royal lord,
Thy wedded handmaid craves of thee a grace.

ALBOVINE
My sovereign bids her bondman what she will.

ROSAMUND
I bid thee mock me not: I may ask thee
Aught, and be heard of any save my lord.

ALBOVINE

Go, friend.

[Exit **NARSETES**.

Speak now. Say first what ails thee?

ROSAMUND
Me?

ALBOVINE
Thy voice was honey-hearted music, sweet
As wine and glad as clarions: not in battle
Might man have more of joy than I to hear it
And feel delight dance in my heart and laugh
Too loud for hearing save its own. Thou rose,
Why did God give thee more than all thy kin
Whose pride is perfume only and colour, this?
Music? No rose but mine sings, and the birds
Hush all their hearts to hearken. Dost thou hear not
How heavy sounds her note now?

ROSAMUND
Sire, not I.
But sire I should not call thee.

ALBOVINE
Surely, no.
I bade thee speak: I did not bid thee sing:
Thou canst not speak and sing not.

ROSAMUND
Albovine,
I had at heart a simple thing to crave
And thought not on thy flatteries—as I think not
Now. Knowest thou not my handmaid Hildegard
Free-born, a noble maiden?

ALBOVINE
And a fair
As ever shone like sundawn on the snows.

ROSAMUND
I had at heart to plead for her with thee.

ALBOVINE
Plead? hast thou found her noble maidenhood
Ignobly turned unmaidenlike? I may not
Lightly believe it.

ROSAMUND

Believe it not at all.
Wouldst thou think shame of me—lightly? She loves
As might a maid whose kin were northern gods
he fairest-faced of warriors Lombard born,
Thine Almachildes.

ALBOVINE

If he loves not her,
More fool is he than warrior even, though war
Have wakened laughter in his eyes, and left
His golden hair fresh gilded, when his hand
Had won the crown that clasps a boy's brows close
With first-born sign of battle.

ROSAMUND

No such fool
May live in such a warrior; if he love not
Some loveliness not hers. No face as bright
Crowned with so fair a Mayflower crown of praise
Lacked ever yet love, if its eyes were set
With all their soul to loveward.

ALBOVINE

Ay?

ROSAMUND

I know not
A man so fair of face. I like him well.
And well he hath served and loves thee.

ALBOVINE

Ay? The boy
Seems winsome then with women.

ROSAMUND

Hildegard
Hath hearkened when he spake of love—it may be,
Lightly.

ALBOVINE

To her shall no man lightly speak.
Thy maiden and our natural kin is she.
Wilt thou speak with him—lightly?

ROSAMUND

If thou wilt,

Gladly.

ALBOVINE
The boy shall wait upon thy will.

[Exit.

ROSAMUND
My heart is heavier than this heat that weighs
With all the weight of June on us. I know not
Why. And the feast is close on us. I would
This night were now to-morrow morn. I know not
Why.

[Enter **ALMACHILDES**.

Ah! What would you?

ALMACHILDES
Queen, our lord the king
Bade me before thee hither.

ROSAMUND
Truth: I know it.
Thou art loved and honoured of our lord the king.
Dost thou, whom honour loves before thy time,
Love?

ALMACHILDES
Ay: thy noble handmaid, Hildegard.
I know not if she love me.

ROSAMUND
Thou shalt know.
But this thou knowest: I may not give thee her.

ALMACHILDES
I would not take her from the Lord God's hand
If hers were given against her will to mine.

ROSAMUND
A man said that: a man fuller than men
Who grip the loveless hands of prisoners. Well
It must be with the bride whose happier hand
Lies fond and fast in thine. Our Hildegard,
Being free and noble as Albovine and we,
Born one with us in race and blood, and thence
Our equal in our sole nobility,

Must well be won by noble works, and love
Whose light is one with honour's.

ALMACHILDES
Queen, may I
Perchance not win it? I know not.

ROSAMUND
Nay, nor I.
Soon may we know; they are entering toward the feast.

[The curtain drawn discovers a banquet, with guests assembled: among them **NARSETES** and
HILDEGARD

[Re-enter **ALBOVINE**.

ALBOVINE
Thine hand: I hold the whitest in the world.
Sit thou, boy, there, beside sweet Hildegard.

[They sit.

Bring me the cup. Queen, thou shalt pledge with me
A health to all this kingdom and its weal
Even from the bowl that here to hold in hand
Assures me lord of Lombardy and thine
By right and might of battle and of God—
The skull that was thy father's: so shalt thou
Drink to me with thy father.

ROSAMUND
Sire, my lord,
The life my sire, who gave thee up his life,
Gave me, and fostered till thou hadst given him death,
Is all now thine. Thy will be done. I drink
To thee, who art all this kingdom and its weal,
All health and honour that of right should be,
With all good things I wish thee. [Drinks.

ALBOVINE
Wish me well,
And God must give me what thou wilt. Good friends,
My warriors and my brethren, hath not he
Given me to wife the best one born of man
And loveliest, and most loving? Silent, sirs?
Wherefore?

ROSAMUND

Thou shouldst not ask it. Bid the cup
Go blithely round.

ALBOVINE
By Christ and Thor, it shall.
What ails the boy there? Almachildes!

ALMACHILDES
King,
Nought ails me.

ALBOVINE
Nor thy maiden?

ALMACHILDES
King, nor her.

ALBOVINE
Fall then to feasting. Bear the cup away.
Some savour of the dust of death comes from it.
Sweet, be not wroth nor sad.

ROSAMUND
I am blithe and fain,
Sire; and I loved thee never more than now.

ALBOVINE
Nor ever I thee. Now I find thee mine,
And now no daughter of mine enemy's.

ROSAMUND
No.
Thou hast no enemy left on earth alive—
No soul unslain that hates thee.

ALBOVINE
That were much.
What man may say it? and least of all may kings.

ROSAMUND
What hast thou done that man should hate thee—man
Or woman?

ALBOVINE
Which of us may answer, Nought?

ROSAMUND
Thou might'st have made me—me, my father's child—

Harlot and slave: thou hast made me wife and queen.

ALBOVINE
Thee have I loved; ay, and myself in thee,
Who hast made me more than king and lord, being thine.

ROSAMUND
Courtesy sets on kings a goldener crown
That sits upon them seemlier.

ALBOVINE
Courtesy!
Truth. Hark thee, boy, and let thy Hildegard
Hearken. Is she, thy queen, a peer of mine?

ALMACHILDES
She wears no crown but heaven's about her head—
No gold that was not born upon her brows
Transfigures or disfigures them. She is not
A peer of thine.

ROSAMUND
He answers well.

ALBOVINE
He answers
Ill—as the spirit of shamelessness might speak.

ALMACHILDES
Shameless are they that lie. I lie not.

ALBOVINE
Boy,
Tempt not the rod.

ALMACHILDES
The rod that man may wield
No man may fear: the slave who fears it is not
Man.

ALBOVINE
Art thou crazed with wine?

ALMACHILDES
Am I thy king?

ALBOVINE
My thrall thou knowest thou art not, or thy tongue

Durst challenge not mine anger.

ROSAMUND
Thrall and free,
Woman and man, yea, queen and king, are born
More wide apart than earth or hell and heaven.
Sirs, let no wrangling breath distune the peace
That shines and glows about us, and discerns
A banquet from a battle. Thou, my lord
Hast bidden away the dust of death which fell
Between us at thy bidding, and is now
Nothing—a dream blown out at waking. Thou,
My lord's young chosen of warriors, be not wroth,
Albeit thy wrath be noble, though my lord
See fit to try my love as gold is tried
By fire: it burns not thee. Strike hand in hand:
Ye have done so after battle.

ALBOVINE
Drink again.
I pledge thee, boy.

ALMACHILDES
I pledge thee, king.

ROSAMUND
My lord,
I am weary at heart, and fain would sleep. Forgive me
That I can sit no more.

ALBOVINE
What ails thee?

ROSAMUND
Nought.
The hot and heavy time of year has bound
About my brows a band of iron. Sire,
Thou wouldst not see me sink aswoon, and mar
The raptures of thy revel.

ALBOVINE
Get thee hence.
Go. God be with thee.

ROSAMUND
God abide with thee.

[Exit with **ATTENDANTS**.

ALBOVINE

This is no feast: I will no more of it. Boy,
Take note, and tempt not so thy bride, albeit
She tempt thee to the trial.

ALMACHILDES

I shall not, king,

ALBOVINE

She will not. Sirs, good night—if night may be
Good. Hardly may the day be, here. And yet
For you it may be—Hildegard and thee.
God give you joy.

ALMACHILDES

God give thee comfort, king.

[Exeunt.

A room in the Queen's apartments.

[Enter **ROSAMUND.**

ROSAMUND

I am yet alive to question if I live
And wonder what may ever bid me die.
But live I will, being yet not dead with thee,
Father. Thou knowest in Paradise my heart.
I feel thy kisses breathing on my lips,
Whereto the dead cold relic of thy face
Was pressed at bidding of thy slayer last night,
And yet they were not withered: nay, they are red
As blood is—blood but newly spilt—not thine.
How good thou wast and sweet of spirit—how dear,
Father! None lives that knew thee now save one,
And none loves me but thou nor thee but I,
That was till yesternight thy daughter: now
That very name is tainted, and my tongue
Tastes poison as I speak it. There is nought
Left in the range and record of the world
For me that is not poisoned: even my heart
Is all envenomed in me. Death is life,
Or priesthood lies that swears it: then I give

The man my husband and thy homicide
Life, if I slay him—the life he gave thee.

[Enter **HILDEGARD**.

Girl,
I sent for thee, I think: stand near me. Child,
Thou art fairer than thou knowest, I doubt: thou art fair
As the awless maidenhood of morning: truth
Should live upon thy lips, though truth were dead
On all men's tongues and women's born save thine.
Dawn lies not when it laughs on us. Thy queen
I am not now: thy friend I would be. Tell
Thy friend if love sleep or awake in thee
Toward any man. Thou art silent. Tell me this,
Dost thou not think, where thought scarce knows itself—
Think in the subtle sense too deep for thought—
That Almachildes loves thee?

HILDEGARD
More than I
Love Almachildes.

ROSAMUND
Thus a maid should speak.
Dost thou love me?

HILDEGARD
Thou knowest it, queen.

ROSAMUND
It lies
Now in thy power to show me more of love
Than ever yet hath man or woman. Swear,
If thou dost love me, thou wilt show it.

HILDEGARD
I swear.

ROSAMUND
By all our fathers' great forsaken gods
Who smiled on all their battles, and by him
Who clomb or crept or leapt upon their throne
And signed us Christian, swear it, then.

HILDEGARD
I swear.

ROSAMUND
What if I bid thee give thyself to shame—
Yield up thy soul and body—play such parts
As shameless fame records of women crowned
Imperial in the tale of lust and Rome?

HILDEGARD
Thou couldst not bid me do it.

ROSAMUND
Thou hast sworn.

HILDEGARD
I have sworn.
Queen, I would do it, and die.

ROSAMUND
Thou shalt not. Yet
This must thou do, and live. Thou shalt not be
Shamed. Thou shalt bid thine Almachildes come
And speak with thee by nightfall. Say, the queen
Will give not up the maiden so beloved
—And truth it is, I love thee—willingly
To the arms of one her husband loves: but were it
Shame, utter shame, that he should wed not her,
The shamefast queen could choose not. Then shall he
Plead. Then shalt thou turn gentler than the snow
That softens at the strong sun's kiss, and yield.
But needs must night be close about your love
And darkness whet your kisses. Light were death.
Hast thou no heart to guess now? Fear not then.
Not thou but I must put on shame. I lack
A hand for mine to grasp and strike with. His
I have chosen.

HILDEGARD
I see but as by lightning. Queen,
What should I do but warn the king—or him?

ROSAMUND
Thou hast sworn. I hold thee by thy word.

HILDEGARD
My Christ,
Help me!

ROSAMUND
No God can break thine oath in twain

And leave thee less than perjured. Thou must bid him
Make thee to-night his bride.

HILDEGARD
I could not say it.

ROSAMUND
Thou shalt, or God shall smite thee down to hell.
What, art thou godless?

HILDEGARD
Art not thou?

ROSAMUND
Not I.
I find him just and gracious, girl: he gives me
My right by might set fast on thine and thee.

HILDEGARD
For love of mercy, queen—for honour's sake,
Bid me not shame myself before a man—
The man I love—who gives me back at least
Honour, if love he gives not.

ROSAMUND
Ay, my maid?
And yet he loves thee, or thy maiden thought
Errs with no gracious error, more than thou
Him?

HILDEGARD
Art thou woman born, to cast me back
My maiden shame for shame upon my face?
I would not say I loved him more than man
Loved ever woman since the light of love
Lit them alive together. Let us be.

ROSAMUND
I will not. Mine are both by God's own gift.
I will not cast it from me. Ye may live
Hereafter happy: never now shall I.

HILDEGARD
Have mercy. Nay, I cannot do it. And thou,
Albeit thine heart be hot with hate as hell,
Couldst say not, nor fold round with fairer speech,
Those foul three words the Egyptian woman said
Who tempted and could tempt not Joseph.

ROSAMUND

No.
He would not hearken. Joseph loved not her
More than thine Almachildes me. But thou
Shalt. Now no more may I debate with thee.
Go.

HILDEGARD

God requite thee!

ROSAMUND

That shall he and I,
Not thou, make proof of. If I plead with him,
I crave of God but wrong's requital. Go.

[Exit **HILDEGARD**.

And yet, God help me! Can I do it? God's will
May no man thwart, or leave his righteousness
Baffled. I would not say, 'My will be done,'
Were God's will not for righteousness as mine,
If right be righteous, wrong be wrong, must be.
How else may God work wrong's requital? I
Must be or none may be his minister.
And yet what righteousness is his to cast
Athwart my way toward right this wrong to me,
A sin against the soul and honour? Why
Must this vile word of YET cross all my thought
Always, a drifting doom or doubt that still
Strikes up and floats against my purpose? God,
Help me to know it! This weapon chosen of me,
This Almachildes, were his face not fair,
Were not his fame bright—were his aspect foul,
His name dishonourable, his line through life
A loathing and a spitting-stock for scorn,
Could I do this? Am I then even as they
Who queened it once in Rome's abhorrent face
An empress each, and each by right of sin
Prostitute? All the life I have lived or loved
Hath been, if snows or seas or wellsprings be,
Pure as the spirit of love toward heaven is—chaste
As children's eyes or mothers'. Though I sinned
As yet my soul hath sinned not, Albovine
Must bear, if God abhor unrighteousness,
The weight of penance heaviest laid on sin,
Shame. Not on me may shame be set, though hell
Take hold upon me dying. I would the deed

Were done, the wreak of wrath were wroken, and I
Dead.

[Enter **ALBOVINE**.

ALBOVINE
Art thou sick at heart to see me?

ROSAMUND
No.

ALBOVINE
Thou art sweet and wise as ever God hath made
Woman. I would not turn thine heart from me
Or set thy spirit against the sense of mine
For more than Rome's old empire.

ROSAMUND
That, albeit
Thou wouldst, be sure thou canst not. God nor man
Could wake within me toward my lord the king
A new strange love or loathing. Fear not this.

ALBOVINE
From thee can I fear nothing. Now I know
How high thy heart is, and how true to me.

ROSAMUND
Thou knowest it now.

ALBOVINE
I know not if I should
Repent me, or repent not, that I tried
A heart so high so sorely—proved so true.

ROSAMUND
Do not repent. I would not have thee now
Repent.

ALBOVINE
By Christ, if God forbade it not,
I would have said within mine own fool's heart,
Of all vile things that fool the soul of man
The vilest and the priestliest hath to name
Repentance. Could it blot one hour's work out,
A wise thing and a manful thing it were,
And profit were it none for priests to preach.
This will I tell thee: what last night befell

Rejoices not but irks me.

ROSAMUND
Let it not
Rejoice nor irk thee. Vex thou not thy soul
With any thought thereon, if none may bid thee
Rejoice: and that were harsh and hard of heart.

ALBOVINE
I will not. Queen and wife, hell durst not say
I do not love thee.

ROSAMUND
Heaven has heard—and I.

ALBOVINE
Forget then all this foolishness, and pray
God may forget it.

ROSAMUND
God forgets as I.

[Exit **ALBOVINE**.

And had repentance helped him? Shall I think
It might have molten in my burning heart
The thrice-retempered iron of resolve?
Yet well it is to know that penitence
Lies further from that frozen heart of his
Than mercy from the tiger's. Ay, God knows,
I had scorned him too had penitence bowed him down
Before me: now I do but hate. I am not
Abased as wholly, so supremely shamed,
As though I had wedded one as hard as he
Who yet might think to soften down with words
What hardly might be cleansed with tears of blood,
The monumental memory graven on steel
That burns the naked spirit of sense within me
Like the ardent sting of keen-edged ice, which makes
The naked flesh feel fire upon it.

[Enter **ALMACHILDES**.

ALMACHILDES
Queen,
I come to crave a word of thee.

ROSAMUND

I hear.

ALMACHILDES
Thou knowest I love thy noble Hildegard:
And rather would I give my soul to burn
Than wrong in thought her flawless maidenhood.
And now she hath told me what I dare not think
Truth. And I dare not think her lips may lie.

ROSAMUND
I have heard. And what is this to me? She hath not
Said—hath not told thee, nor wouldst thou believe—
That I have breathed a lie upon her lips
Or taught them shamelessness by lesson?

ALMACHILDES
No.
But she came forth from thee to me—from thee—
And spake with quivering mouth and quailing eyes
And face whose fire turned ashen, and again
Rekindling from that ashen agony
Flamed, what no heart could think to hear her speak,
Mine least of all, who love her.

ROSAMUND
Ay?

ALMACHILDES
Not she,
I know it as sure as night is known from day
And surelier than I know mine own soul's truth,
Spake what she spake in broken bursts of breath
Out of her own heart and its love for me.

ROSAMUND
Didst thou so answer her?

ALMACHILDES
I might not well
Answer at all.

ROSAMUND
Poor maid, she hath loved amiss.
Belike she thought to find in thee a man's
Love.

ALMACHILDES
That she hath found; nought meaner than a man's;

No wolfish lust of ravenous insolence
To soil and spoil her of her noblest name.

ROSAMUND
I do not ask thee what she said. I know.

ALMACHILDES
I knew thou didst.

ROSAMUND
To make your bridal sure
She bade thee make thy bride of her to-night.

ALMACHILDES
She bade me as a slave might bid the scourge
Fall.

ROSAMUND
Such a scourge no slave might shrink from; nay,
No free-born woman, Almachildes.

ALMACHILDES
Queen,
I crave thy queenly mercy though I say
My maid, my bride that will be, shrank, and showed
In all the rosebright anguish of her face
A shuddering shame that wrung my heart. And thou
Hast surely set thereon that seal of shame.
I know it as thou dost.

ROSAMUND
Ay, and more she said,
Surely: she said I would not yield her up
To the arms of one my husband loves and holds
Honoured at heart—I hate my husband so,
She told thee—were the need avoidable
Save by her sacrifice to shame.

ALMACHILDES
Thou knowest
All, as I knew, and lacked not from thy lips
Confession.

ROSAMUND
Warrior though thou be, and boy
Though my lord call thee, brainless art thou not—
No sword with man's face carven on the heft
For mockery more than truth or help in fight.

I do not and I durst not play with thee.
Thy bride spake truth: I knew not she might need
So much of truth to tempt thee toward her. Now
Thou knowest, and I know. If this imminent night
Make not thy darkling bride of her, by day
Thy bride she may be never. She hath sworn.

ALMACHILDES
Why wouldst thou shame her?

ROSAMUND
Shamed she cannot be
If thou be found not shameless. Plead no more
Against thine own love's surety. Doubt thou not
I wish thee well, and love her. Make not thou
Out of her shamefast maidenhood and fear
A sword to cleave your happiness in twain.
What if some oath constrain me, sworn in haste,
Infrangible for shame's sake, sealed in heaven
Inevitable? Ask now no more of me.
Nightfall is here upon us. Nought on earth
May set the season of your bridal back
If thou be true as she must. Wait awhile
Here till a sign be sent thee—till a bell
Strike softly from this chamber here at hand.
I have sworn to her she shall not see thy face,
So sore she prayed she might not: and for thee
I swore that ere the darkling air grew grey
Thou shouldst arise and leave her, and behold
Thy midnight bride but when thou art bidden again
To meet her here to-morrow. Strange it were,
More strange than aught of all, that thou shouldst prove
Dishonourable: and except thou be, these things
Must all be wrought in this wise, lest her oath
And mine, at peril of her soul and life,
By passionate forgetfulness of thine
Disloyally be broken. Swear to us now
Thou wilt not break our oath and thine, or think
To look to-night upon thy bride.

ALMACHILDES
I swear.

ROSAMUND
I take thine oath. I bid not thee take heed
That I or thou or each of us at once,
Couldst thou play false, may die: I bid thee think
Thy bride will die, shamed. Swear me not again

She shall not: all our trust is set on thee.
What eyes and ears are keen about us here
Thou knowest not. Love, my love and thine for her,
Shall deafen and shall blind them. Be but thou
A bridegroom blind and dumb—speak soft as love,
And ask not answer louder than a sigh—
And when to-morrow sets thy bride and thee
Here face to face again, thy soul shall stand
Amazed: thy joy shall turn to wonder. This
Thy queen, whose power may seal her promise fast,
Swears for thine oath again to thee. Good night.

[Exit.

ALMACHILDES
I cannot think I live. Our Sigurd loved not
Brynhild as I love her, and even this hour
Shall make us great as they. No spell to break,
No fire to pass, divides us. Blind and dumb,
Love knows, would I be ever while I live
For love's sake rather than forego the joy
That makes one godlike power of spirit and sense,
One godhead born of manhood. God requite
The queen who loves my love and cares for me
Thus! How may man or God requite her? Ah!

[Bell rings softly from without.

There sounds the note that opens heaven on me,
And how should man dare heaven? But love may dare. [Exit.

ACT III

An eastward room in the Palace.

[Enter **ALBOVINE**.

ALBOVINE
This sun—no sun like ours—burns out my soul.
I would, when June takes hold on us like fire,
The wind could waft and whirl us northward: here
The splendour and the sweetness of the world
Eat out all joy of life or manhood. Earth
Is here too hard on heaven—the Italian air
Too bright to breathe, as fire, its next of kin,
Too keen to handle. God, whoe'er God be,

Keep us from withering as the lords of Rome—
Slackening and sickening toward the imperious end
That wiped them out of empire! Yea, he shall.

[Enter **HILDEGARD**.

HILDEGARD
The queen would wait upon your majesty.

ALBOVINE
Bid her come in. And tell her ere she come
I wait upon her will.

[Exit **HILDEGARD**.]

What would she now?

[Enter **ROSAMUND**.

By Christ, how fair thou art! I never saw thee
So like the sun in heaven: no rose on earth
Might think to match thee.

ROSAMUND
All I am is thine.

ALBOVINE
Mine? God might come from heaven to worship thee.
Thine eyes outlighten all the stars: thy face
Leaves earth no flower to worship.

ROSAMUND
How should earth
Worship her children? Nought it is in me,
My lord's dear love it is, that makes me seem
Fair.

ALBOVINE
How thou liest thou knowest not. Rosamund,
What hast thou done to be so beautiful?

ROSAMUND
The sun has left thine eyes half blind.

ALBOVINE
I dare not
Kiss thee, or stare straight-eyed against the sun.

ROSAMUND

Kiss me. Who knows how long the lord of life
May spare us time for kissing? Life and love
Are less than change and death.

ALBOVINE

What ghosts are they?
So sweet thou never wast to me before.
The woman that is God—the God that is
Woman—the sovereign of the soul of man,
Our fathers' Freia, Venus crowned in Rome,
Has lent my love her girdle; but her lips
Have robbed the red rose of its heart, and left
No glory for the flower beyond all flowers
To bid the spring be glad of.

ROSAMUND

Summer and spring
May cleanse and heal the heart of man no more
Than winter may, or withering autumn. Sire,
Husband and lord, I have a woful word
To speak against a man beloved of thee,
A man well worth all glory man may give—
Against thine Almachildes.

ALBOVINE

Has the boy
Transgressed again in awless heat of speech
And kindled wrath in thee against him—thee,
Who stood'st between my wrath and him?

ROSAMUND

I would
His were no more transgression than of speech.
He hath wronged—I bid thee ask of me no more—
A noble maiden. Till her shame be healed,
Her name is dead upon my lips and his,
Who is yet not all ignoble.

ALBOVINE

He shall die
Except he wed her, and she will to wed.

ROSAMUND

That surely will she.

ALBOVINE

Bid him hither.

ROSAMUND
See,
There strides he through the sunshine toward the shade.
How light and high he steps! He sees thee. Bid him—
Beckon him in.

ALBOVINE
He knows mine eye. He comes.

ROSAMUND
Obedient as a hound is.

ALBOVINE
As a man
That knows the law of loyal manhood.

ROSAMUND
Ay?
God send it be so.

[Enter **ALMACHILDES**.

ALMACHILDES
Queen and king, I am here.
What would you?

ALBOVINE
Truth. Hast thou not borne thyself
Toward any soul on earth disloyally
Ever?

ALMACHILDES
Never.

ALBOVINE
I would not say thou liest.

ALMACHILDES
Do not: the lie should burn thy lips up, king.

ALBOVINE
Thou hast wrought no wrong toward man or woman?

ALMACHILDES
None.

ALBOVINE

Speak thou: thou hast heard him answer me.

ROSAMUND
I have heard.
No wrong it may be with the serfs of hell
To cast upon a woman for a curse
Shame: to defile the spirit and shrine of love,
Put out the sunlike eyes of maidenhood
And leave the soul dismantled. Has not he
So sinned?—Hast thou wrought no such work as this?
The king has heard thy silence.

ALMACHILDES
Queen and king,
I have done no wrong, but right. I have chosen my bride,
And made her mine by gentle grace of hers
Lest wrong should come between us. Now no man
May think to unwed us: king nor queen may cross
This wedded love of ours: no thwart or stay
May sunder us till heaven and earth turn hell.

ALBOVINE
I deemed not thee dishonourable: and thy queen
Now knows thee true as I did. Rosamund,
Forgive and give him back his bride.

ROSAMUND
I will,
King.

ALBOVINE
Boy, thy queen hath shown thee grace; be thou
Thankful. I leave thee here to yield her thanks.

[Exit.

ALMACHILDES
Queen, I would die to serve and thank thee.

ROSAMUND
Die?
So young and glad and glorious? Thou shalt not
Die. Was thy bride's face bright to look upon
When last night's moon and stars illumined it?

ALMACHILDES
Thou knowest I might not look upon it.

ROSAMUND
No.
Thou hast never loved before?

ALMACHILDES
I have loathed, not loved,
The loveless harlots clasped of all the camp:
I have followed wars and visions all my days
Even till my love's eyes lit and stung to life
The soul within my body. Till I loved,
I knew not woman.

ROSAMUND
Now thou knowest. This love
Is no good lord—no gentle god—no soft
Saviour. Thou knowest perchance thy bride's name—hers
Whose body and soul were one but now with thine?

ALMACHILDES
How should not I? What darkling light is this
That burns and broods and lightens in thine eyes,
Queen?

ROSAMUND
Hildegard it was not.

ALMACHILDES
Art not thou—
Or am not I—sun-smitten through the brain
By this mad might of midsummer? Who was it
That slept or slept not with me while the night
Was more than noon and more than heaven? What name
Was hers who made me godlike?

ROSAMUND
Rosamund.

ALMACHILDES
Thine? was it thou? It was not.

ROSAMUND
It was I.

ALMACHILDES
Does the sun stand in heaven? Or stands it fast
As when God bade it halt on high? My life
Is broken in me.

ROSAMUND
Nay, fair sir, not yet.
Thy life is now mine—as the ring I wear
That seals my hand a wife's. Die thou shalt not,
But slay, and live.

ALMACHILDES
Slay whom?

ROSAMUND
Thy lord and mine.

ALMACHILDES
I had rather go down quick to hell.

ROSAMUND
I know it.
I leave thee not the choice. Keep thou thy hand
Bloodless, and Hildegard, whom yet I love,
Dies, and in fire, the harlot's death of shame.
Last night she lured thee hither. Hate of me,
Because of late I smote her, being in wrath
Forgetful of her noble maidenhood,
Stung her for shame's sake to take hands with shame.
This if I swear, may she unswear it? Thou
Canst not but say she bade thee seek her. She
Lives while I will, as Albovine and thou
Live by my grace and mercy. Live, or die.
But live thou shalt not longer than her death,
Her death by burning, if thou slay not him.
I see my death shine in thine eyes: I see
My present death inflame them. That were not
Her surety, Almachildes. Thou shouldst know me
Now. Though thou slay me, this may save not her.
My lines are laid about her life, and may not
By breach of mine be broken.

ALMACHILDES
God must be
Dead. Such a thing as thou could never else
Live.

ROSAMUND
That concerns not thee nor me. Be thou
Sure that my will and power to serve it live.
Lift now thine eyes to look upon thy lord.

[Re-enter **ALBOVINE**.

ALBOVINE
By this time hath he thanked thee not enough?

ROSAMUND
More hath he given than thanks.

ALBOVINE
What more may be?

ROSAMUND
His plighted faith to heal the wrong he wrought
Faithfully.

ALBOVINE
Boy, strike then thy hand in mine.
Thou art loyal as I knew thee.

ALMACHILDES
King, I may not
Touch hands with thee.

ALBOVINE
Thou art false, then, ha? Thou hast lied?

ALMACHILDES
King, till the wrong I have wrought be wreaked or healed
I clasp not hands with honour. Nay, and then
Perchance I may not.

ALBOVINE
Boy I called thee: child
I call thee now. But, boy, the child thou art
Is noble as our sires.

ALMACHILDES
Would God it were!

[Exit.

ALBOVINE
What ails him?

ROSAMUND
Love and shame.

ALBOVINE
No more than these?

ROSAMUND
Enough are they to darken death and life.

ALBOVINE
Thou art less than gentle towards his love and him.

ROSAMUND
I would not speak ungently. Her I love,
Poor child, and him I hate not.

ALBOVINE
Thou shalt live
To love him too.

ROSAMUND
This heaviness of heat
Kills love and hate and life in me. I know not
Aught lovesome save the sweet brief death of sleep.

ALBOVINE
I am weary as thou. Good night we may not say—
Good noon I bid thee. Sleep shall heal us.

ROSAMUND
Ay;
No healing and no help for life on earth
Hath God or man found out save death and sleep.

[Exeunt.

ACT IV

The same Scene.

[Enter **ALMACHILDES** and **HILDEGARD**.

HILDEGARD
Hast thou forgiven me?

ALMACHILDES
I have not forgiven
God.

HILDEGARD
Wilt thou slay thy soul and mine?

ALMACHILDES
Wilt thou
Madden me? God hath given us up to her
Who is deadlier than the fiery fang of death—
Us, innocent and loyal.

HILDEGARD
Nay, if I
Forgive her love of thee—though this be hard,
Canst thou forgive not?

ALMACHILDES
Sweet, for thee and me
Remains no rescue save by death or flight
From worse than flight or death is.

HILDEGARD
Worse is nought
But shame: and how may shame take hold on us,
On us who have sinned not? Me she bound to play thee
False, and betray thee to her arms: I might not
Choose, though my heart should rend itself in twain
And cleave with ravenous anguish: yet I live.
Vex not thy soul too sorely: me, not her,
Thy spirit embraced, thine arms and lips made thine
Me, not my darkling wraith, my changeling foe,
My thief of love, our traitress. This I bid thee,
Forget thy fear and shame to have wronged me: night
Breeds treacherous dreams that can but poison day
If thought be found so base a fool as dares
Fear. Did I doubt thy love of me, I durst not
Live or look back upon thee.

ALMACHILDES
Wilt thou then
Fly?

HILDEGARD
Dost thou know what flight means—thou?
It means
Fear. And is fear a new-born friend of thine?

ALMACHILDES
God help us! if he live, and hate not man—
If Satan be not God. We will not fly.

[Enter **ALBOVINE** and **ROSAMUND**.

ALBOVINE
Fly? What should love at height of happiness
Or youth at height of honour fear and fly?
Would ye take wing for heaven? take shame on earth
To wed in peace and honour?

ALMACHILDES
No, my king.
No, surely.

ROSAMUND
Weep not, maiden. Dost not thou,
Man, that we thought her bridegroom sealed of love,
Love her?

ALMACHILDES
No saint loved ever God as I
Her.

ROSAMUND
And betray her to shame thou wouldst not?
See,
My lord, the silent answer flash aloud
From cheek and eye a goodly witness. Thou,
My maiden, dost thou love not him? Nay, speak.

HILDEGARD
I cannot say it—I cannot strive to say.

ROSAMUND
Thou shalt. Are all we not fast bound in love—
My lord and thine, my maiden and her queen,
A fourfold chain of faith twice linked of love?
Speak: let not shame find place where shame is none.

HILDEGARD
I will not. King and queen and God shall hear.
I love him as our songs of old time say
Men have been loved of women akin to gods
By blood as they by spirit, albeit in me
Nought lives that woman or man or God could say
Were worth his love, if mine by grace of love
Be found not all unworthy. Mine am I
No more: mine own in no wise now, but his
To save or slay, to cherish or cast out,
Crown and discrown, abase and comfort. Shame
Were more to me than honour if his will

It were that shame should clothe me round, and life
Were the only death left fearful if he bade me
Die. Could his love be turned from me, and set
On one less loving but more fair than I,
A thrall more base than treason or a queen
Too high for shame to brand her shameful, even
Though sin had stamped and signed her foul as fraud
And loathsome as a masked adulterous lie,
Hers would I make him if I might, and yield
To her the hatefullest of hell-born things
The man found lovelier by my love than heaven.

ROSAMUND
Great love is this to brag of: great and strange.

HILDEGARD
Love is no braggart: lust and fraud and hate
Vaunt their vile strength when shame unveils them: love
Vaunts not itself. I spake not uncompelled,
And blushed not out the avowal.

ALBOVINE
Boy, I held
And hold thee noblest of my lords of war,
And worthier than thine elders born and tried
Ere battle found thee ripe and glad at heart
To stem and swim the tide of spears: but this
I know not if thou be or any man
Be worthy of.

ALMACHILDES
Of all men born on earth
I am most unworthy of it. None might be
Worthy.

ROSAMUND
He weeps: thy boy is humble.

ALMACHILDES
Queen,
I weep not. Shamed with no ignoble shame
Thou seest me: but I weep not. Yea, God knows,
Humbled I am, and humble; not to thee.

ALBOVINE
Chafe not: and thou, queen though thou be, and mine,
Tempt not a true man's wrath with words that bear
Fangs keener than thou knowest of.

ROSAMUND
King, henceforth,
Being warned, I will not. Dangerous as the sea
A true man's wrath is—and a true man's love:
A woman's hath no peril in it: her tears
Wash wrath and peril away.

ALBOVINE
I have never seen thee
Weep.

ROSAMUND
How should I weep—I, thy wife?

ALBOVINE
I have heard thee
Laugh; and thy smiles were always bright as fire.

ROSAMUND
Well were it with me—ay, and reason found
For me to live and do the living world
Some service—could my husband warm thereat
His heart as winter-stricken hands in frost
Are warmed at winter fires.

ALBOVINE
No need, no need:
The sun thou art warms all our year with love,
And leaves no chill on winter.

ROSAMUND
Albovine,
Love now secludes us not from sight of man—
From sight of this my maiden and the man
Who shines but as the battle's boy for thee
But lives for me my maiden's lover—true
As truth is—Almachildes.

ALBOVINE
How thy lips
Hang lingering on his name as though 'twere thou
That loved him! Thou shouldst love thy maiden well.

ROSAMUND
As she loves me I love her. Hildegard,
Leave us. Thou knowest I love thee.

HILDEGARD
Queen, I know.

[Exit.

ALBOVINE
What ails the boy? what rapturous agony
Torments and glorifies his glance at her
As with delight in torture? Cheer thee, man:
Thou art not thus all unworthy.

ROSAMUND
Spare him, king.
A king may guess not how a man's heart yearns
With all unkingly sense of love and shame
Not all unmanly.

ALBOVINE
Shame is none to be
Loved, and to deem that love exceeds our due
Who may not well deserve it. Sick at heart
He seems, and should be gladder than the sea
When wind and sun strike life in it.

ALMACHILDES
I am not
So stricken, king. I thank thy care of me.

ALBOVINE
Heart-stricken or shame-stricken art thou?

ROSAMUND
King,
Spare him. Thou knowest not love like his. It burns
And rends and wrings the spirit.

ALBOVINE
No. And thou,
Dost thou then?

ROSAMUND
Eyes and heart and sense are mine
As weak and strong as woman's can but be;
As weak in strength and strong in weakness. Men,
Being wise, and mightier than their mates on earth,
Need no such knowledge born of inborn pain
As quickens all the spirit of sense in us.
Worms know what eagles know not.

ALBOVINE

Like enough.
Rede me no redes and riddles. Never yet
I have loved thee more, and yet I have loved thee well,
Than now that loving-kindness borne toward love
Makes thee so gracious, pleading for it.

ROSAMUND

Love
Sees all things lovely: thine, if praise there be,
Not mine the praise is: thee, not me, these twain
Must love and worship as their lord of love.

ALBOVINE

Well, God be good to them and thee and me!
I would this fierce Italian June were dead,
So hard it weighs upon me.

ROSAMUND

Now not long
Shall we sustain or sink aswoon from it:
It has but left a day or two to die.

ALBOVINE

And well were that, if summer died with June.
Two red months more must set on sense and soul
The branding-iron stamped of summer: nay,
The sea is here no sea to cherish man:
It brings no choral comfort back with tides
That surge and sink and swell and chime and change
And lighten life with music where the breath
Dies and revives of night and day.

ROSAMUND

Be thou
Content: a God hath driven us hither.

ALBOVINE

Yea:
A God of death and fire and strife, whose hand
Is heavy on my spirit. Be not ye
Troubled, if peace be with you.

ROSAMUND

Peace to thee.

[Exit **ALBOVINE.**

Now follow: smite him now: thou art strong, but yet
Thy king is stronger—mightier thewed than thou.
Thou couldst not slay him in fight.

ALMACHILDES
I cannot slay him
Thus.

ROSAMUND
Canst thou slay thy bride by fire? He dies,
Or she dies, bound against the stake. His death
Were the easier. Follow him: save her: strike but once.

ALMACHILDES
I cannot. God requite thee this! I will. [Exit.

ROSAMUND
And I will see it. And, father, thou shalt see.

[Exit.

ACT V

The Banqueting-hall.

Enter **ALBOVINE** and **ROSAMUND**.

ALBOVINE
This June makes babes of men; last night I deemed
When thou hadst wished me peace as I passed forth
A footfall pressed behind me soft and fast,
And turning toward it I beheld nought: thee
I saw, and Almachildes hard at hand
Turned back toward thee: nought stranger: yet my heart
Sprang, and sank back. I laughed against myself,
That manhood should be girlish, when the heat
Burns life half out within us. Even thine eyes,
Like stars before the wind that brings the cloud,
Look fainter. Ere they fill the banquet full
And bid the guests about us where we sit,
Tell me if aught be worse than well with thee.

ROSAMUND
Nought.

ALBOVINE
Wilt thou swear it, sweet?

ROSAMUND
By what thou wilt—
By God and man—by hell and earth and heaven.
I know what ails thy loyal heart of love
And binds thy tongue for fear to bid me know.
The cup we drank of when we feasted last
Tastes bitter on it yet. Thou wilt not bid me
Pledge thee therein again. If I bid thee,
Pledge me thou shalt—and seal thy pardon.

ALBOVINE
Be not
Too sweet for woman.

ROSAMUND
Cross me not in this.

ALBOVINE
Mine old fast friend Narsetes hath my word
Plighted. All funeral reverence shall inter
The royal relic, and all thought therewith
Of strife between thy father's child and me
Or less than love and honour.

ROSAMUND
Nay, my lord,
Let the dead thing live as a lifelong sign
Of perfect plight in love and union. This
Were no dishonour done to fatherhood
But honour shown to wedlock. Here is spread
The feast, the bride-feast of my love and thine,
Whereat the cup of death shall serve our lips
To drink forgetfulness of all but love.
Herein thou shalt not thwart me.

ALBOVINE
God forbid.

ROSAMUND
God hath forbidden: and God shall be obeyed.
Bid thy Narsetes play the cup-bearer,
And I will pour the wine: my hand shall fill
The sacramental draught of love that seals
Our eucharist of wedlock.

ALBOVINE
Yea, I know
To drink with thee is even to drink with God.
Thou art good as any God was ever.

ROSAMUND
Ay?
We know not till we die.

ALBOVINE
Thou art wise and true
As ever maid was born of the oldworld north
In the oldworld years of legend. Bid Narsetes
Bring thee the chalice: thou shalt mix the draught
Whence we will drink life, if true love be life,
Even from the lipless mouth of bone that speaks
Death.

ROSAMUND
I will mix it well with honey and herb
Sweet as the mead our fathers drank, and dreamed
Their gods so drank in heaven—draughts deep and strong
As life is strong and death is deep. I go
To bid Narsetes hither.

[Exit.

ALBOVINE
Nay, by God,
Whoever God be, never Christ or Thor
Beheld or blessed a nobler wife, whose love
Was found through proof of purity by fire
More like our northern stars and snows and suns,
And sane in strong sufficiency of soul
As womanhood by godhead from the womb
Elected and exalted.

[Enter **NARSETES**.

NARSETES
King, thy wife
Hath given me back thy message given her.

ALBOVINE
Ay?
And thou hast given her back my cup, then?

NARSETES

King,
I have given it. Loth to give it if I were,
Ye know: she knows as thou: thou knowest as she.

ALBOVINE
What ails thee to distaste thy duty? Man,
Thou shouldst be glad, being loyal. Knowest thou not
Her will it was that we should pledge therein
To-night, this hour, our lifelong love, and seal it
More surely so than priest or prayer can seal?

NARSETES
Her will it was, I know, not thine. I would
Thou hadst not yielded up to hers thy will.

ALBOVINE
Thou liest: I have not yielded it: I have given
Love, willing as the springtide sea gives up
Her will to the eastern sea-wind's.

NARSETES
Love should give
No more than love should crave of love: and this
Is such a gift as hate might crave of death
Or priests of God when angered.

ALBOVINE
Hark thee, man.
Thou art old, and when I loved thee first and found thee
My lord and leader down the ways of war,
My master born by right of manfulness
And steersman through the surf of battle, time
Gaped as a gulf between us: sire and son
We might be: now I bid thee hold thy peace,
Lest all these memories perish, and their death
Give life more strong than theirs to wrath, and leave thee
Shelterless as a waif of the air when storm
Drives bird and beast to deathward. What I bade thee
I bid thee do, and leave me.

NARSETES
King, I go.

[Exit.

ALBOVINE
What, have I played the Berserk with my friend?
So should not kings. What meant he? Men wax old,

And age eats out the natural sense of love
Which gives the soul sight of such nobler things
As trust may see by grace of truth more fair
Than doubt would fear to dream of. Rosamund
Knows more by might of faith and love than he.
And yet I would, and yet I would not, fool
As even in mine own eyes I am, she had not
Given me this proof, desired of me this sign,
How clear her soul is toward me save of love,
To attest her pardon of me. Would it were
Sunrise to-morrow!

[Enter **ALMACHILDES** and **HILDEGARD**.

Whence come these, to bring
Sunrise about me? Nay, I bade you be
Here. Does thy memory too not fail thee, boy,
Burnt out by stress of summer

ALMACHILDES
No.

ALBOVINE
Nor hers?

HILDEGARD
How might it, king? Thou art good to us.

ALBOVINE
All things born
Seem good to lovers in their spring of love,
And all men should be. Maiden, God doth well
To give us foresight of the sight of heaven
By looking in such eyes as love like thine
Kindles and veils for love's sake. Fain was I
To see my boy's bride and her bridegroom here
Before the feast broke in on us, and bless
Their love with mine—if mine be blessing.

HILDEGARD
Sire,
As the earth gives thanks in spring for the April sun
I would and cannot yield you thanks for this.

ALMACHILDES
I cannot thank at all. I cannot thank
God.

ALBOVINE

Art thou mazed with love? For her thou canst not
Thank God? What feverish doubt of love or life
Crazes or cramps thy spirit?

ALMACHILDES

I cannot say.
My heart, if any heart be left in me,
Is as it was not thankless: yet, my king,
I know not how to thank thee.

ALBOVINE

Thank me not:
I did not bid thee thank me. Love thy love,
And God be with you: so may God be found
Thank worthier. Keep some heart in thee awhile
For God's and her sake.

ALMACHILDES

All I may I will.

[Re-enter **ROSAMUND**, followed by **NARSETES** and **GUESTS**.

ALBOVINE

Sit, friends and warriors: thou, my boy, next me,
And by my wife thy bride. This night, that leaves
But two days more for June to burn and live,
Plights with my queen's troth mine in life and death
This last one time for ever, in the cup
Whence none shall drink hereafter. Not in scorn,
Sirs, but in honour now the draught is pledged
Between us, ere this relic stand enshrined
And hallowed as a saint's on the altar. Queen,
I drink to thee.

ROSAMUND

I thank thee. Good Narsetes,
Give him the chalice. Women slain by fire
Thirst not as I to pledge thee.

[As **ALBOVINE** is about to take the cup, **ALMACHILDES** rises and stabs him.

ALBOVINE

Thou, my boy?

[Dies.

ROSAMUND

I. But he hears not. Now, my warrior guests,
I drink to the onward passage of his soul
Death. Had my hand turned coward or played me false,
This man that is my hand, and less than I
And less than he blood guilty, this my death
Had been my husband's: now he has left it me.

[Drinks.

How innocent are all but he and I
No time is mine to tell you. Truth shall tell.
I pardon thee, my husband: pardon me.

[Dies.

NARSETES
Let none make moan. This doom is none of man's.

Algernon Charles Swinburne – A Short Biography

Algernon Charles Swinburne was born at 7 Chester Street, Grosvenor Place, in London, on April 5th, 1837. He was the eldest of six children born to Captain Charles Henry Swinburne and Lady Jane Henrietta, daughter of the 3rd Earl of Ashburnham, a wealthy Northumbrian family.

Swinburne spent his early years at East Dene in Bonchurch, on the Isle of Wight. As a child, Swinburne was nervous and frail, but also imbued with a nervous energy and fearlessness almost to the point of recklessness.

He was schooled at Eton College from 1849 to 1853.   It was here that he first began to write poetry. He excelled at languages and whilst still at Eton won first prizes in both French and Italian.

From Eton he moved to Oxford where he attended at Balliol College from 1856.   Here he met friends to whom he became closely attached, among them Dante Gabriel Rossetti, William Morris and Edward Burne-Jones, who in 1857, were painting their Arthurian murals on the walls of the Oxford Union.   At Oxford Swinburne was mentored by Benjamin Jowett, the master of Balliol College, who recognised his poetic talent and, intervening on his behalf, tried to keep him from being expelled when he celebrated the Italian patriot Orsini, and his failed attempt on the life of Napoleon III in 1858. Swinburne had to leave the Universcity for a few months due to this but returned in May, 1860 but never received a degree.

Summers were usually spent at Capheaton Hall in Northumberland, the house of his grandfather, Sir John Swinburne, 6th Baronet, who had a famous library and was himself President of the Literary and Philosophical Society in Newcastle upon Tyne.

Swinburne proudly considered himself a native of Northumberland and this is reflected in poems such as the intensely patriotic 'Northumberland' and 'Grace Darling'. He enjoyed riding across the moors and was, it was said, a daring horseman, as he moved 'through honeyed leagues of the northland border', as he remembered the Scottish border in his Recollections.

In the period from 1857 to 1860, Swinburne was one of a number of Pre-Raphaelite's who visited and became part of Lady Pauline Trevelyan's intellectual circle at Wallington Hall, a few miles west of Morpeth in Northumberland.

After leaving college, he moved to London and began his career in earnest as well as becoming a constant visitor to the Rossetti's house.   To Rossetti Swinburne was his 'little Northumbrian friend', an affectionate reference to Swinburne's small stature—a mere five foot four. Whatever Swinburne lacked in height he made up for in poetic talent.   However, with the burden of such great talent came the unveiling of a dark side that was to cause him pain and would, at times, threaten his very existence with all manner of self-inflicted pains through drink, drugs and sado-machoism.

In 1860 Swinburne published two verse dramas; The Queen Mother and Rosamond but it would not be until 1865 that Swinburne would achieve literary success with Atalanta in Calydon.

In 1861, Swinburne visited Menton on the French Riviera to recover from the effects of yet another period of excess use of alcohol, staying at the Villa Laurenti. From Menton, Swinburne then travelled on to Italy, where he journeyed widely.

After Elizabeth Rossetti's death from suicide in 1862, he and Rossetti moved to Tudor House at 16 Cheyne Walk in Chelsea. The stories that survive from his year with Rossetti are typical Swinburne.   In one, Rossetti once had to tell him to keep down the noise — he and a boyfriend had been sliding naked down the bannisters and disturbing Rossetti's painting. He took a sardonic delight in what the critic and biographer, Cecil Lang, calls "Algernonic exaggeration": When people began to talk scathingly about his homosexuality and other sexual proclivities, he circulated a story that he had engaged in pederasty and bestiality with a monkey — and then eaten it. How many of the stories were true and how many invented is unclear. Oscar Wilde called him "a braggart in matters of vice, who had done everything he could to convince his fellow citizens of his homosexuality and bestiality without being in the slightest degree a homosexual or a bestialiser."

In December 1862, Swinburne accompanied Scott and his guests on a trip to Tynemouth. Scott writes in his memoirs that, as they walked by the sea, Swinburne declaimed the as yet unpublished 'Hymn to Proserpine' and 'Laus Veneris' in his lilting intonation, while the waves 'were running the whole length of the long level sands towards Cullercoats and sounding like far-off acclamations'.

Swinburne possessed a curious combination of frail health and strength. He was small and slightly built, but an excellent swimmer and the first to climb Culver Cliff on the Isle of Wight. He had an extremely excitable disposition: people who met him described him as a "demoniac boy" who would go skipping about the room declaiming poetry at the top of his voice. In this as in many things, moderation was not the standard for him.   Excess was.   Once or twice he had fits, thought to be epileptic, in public; but he made this condition much worse by drinking past excess to unconsciousness. More than once he was delivered to the door in the small of the night, dead drunk. Throughout the 1860s and '70s he rode an alcoholic cycle of dissolution, collapse, drying out at home in the country, then returning to London where he would begin the cycle all over again.

His mania for masochism, particularly flagellation, most probably started in early childhood at Eton and was encouraged by his later friendships with Richard Monckton Milnes (one of Tennyson's fellow Apostles), who introduced him to the works of the Marquis de Sade, and Richard Burton, the Victorian explorer and adventurer. Swinburne was an alcoholic and algolagniac (a desire for sexual gratification through inflicting pain on oneself or others; sadomasochism). He found life difficult, unfulfilling but still his poetic talents pushed to the fore.

Although Swinburne continued to publish some works in periodicals in 1865 he was granted recognition by both public and critics with Atalanta in Calydon written in the style of a classical Greek tragedy.

There followed "Laus Veneris" and Poems and Ballads (1866), with their sexually charged passages, absolutely decadent for polite Victorian society, which were attacked all the more violently as a result. The poems written in homage of Sappho of Lesbos such as "Anactoria" and "Sapphics" were especially savaged. The volume also contained poems such as "The Leper," "Laus Veneris," and "St Dorothy" which evoke both Swinburne's and a general Victorian fascination with the Middle Ages, and are explicitly mediaeval in style, tone and construction. With its publication came instant notoriety. He was now identified with indecent and decadent themes and the precept of art for art's sake.

Swinburne's meeting in 1867 with his long-time hero Mazzini, the Italian patriot living in England in exile, was the beginning of a poetical journey that now became more serious and more engaged with serious thought, initially leading to the political poems in the volume Songs Before Sunrise.

Also in 1867 he was introduced to Adah Isaacs Menken, the American actress, poet and circus rider, whose main fame seemed to be riding naked on a horse (in fact she wore tight nude coloured clothing) for her performance in the melodrama Mazeppa (itself based on a poem by Lord Byron). Although they had a short affair Adah's quote implies that Swinburne was not ready for a relationship that did not involve some self-sabotage; "I can't make him understand that biting's no use."

In 1879, with Swinburne nearly dead from alcoholism and dissolution, his legal advisor Theodore Watts-Dunton took him in, and was gradually successful in getting him to adapt to a healthier lifestyle. Swinburne lived the rest of his life at Watts-Dunton's house. He saw less and less of his old bohemian friends, who thought him a prisoner at The Pines, but his growing deafness also accounts for some of his decreased sociability. By now Swinburne was 42, and was moving from a young man of rebelliousness to a figure of social respectability. It was said of Watts-Dunton that he saved the man and killed the poet.

It is clear that Swinburne had an addictive personality, and clearly incapable of moderation in his pursuit of any chosen vices. This, of course, would both nourish and perhaps sabotage his poetic career. His poetry follows the somewhat clichéd pattern of early flourish and later decline; indeed some of the fresher pieces in the second and third series of Poems and Ballads (published in 1878 and 1889) were actually written during his days at Oxford. Nevertheless, his last collection, A Channel Passage, has some beautiful poems, including "The Lake of Gaube."

He is best remembered as the supreme technician in metre, with a versatility which exceeds even Tennyson's, but which lacks a corresponding emotional range. His obsessions are not widely enough shared; and if he cannot shock us by the strangeness of his desires nor the shrillness of his anti-theistical exclamations, often what remains is not enough to fully engage with the audience.

Swinburne is considered a poet of the decadent school, although he perhaps professed to more vice than he actually indulged in to advertise his deviance. Common gossip of the time reported that he also had a deep crush on the explorer Sir Richard Francis Burton, despite the fact that Swinburne himself abhorred travel.   Fact and fiction are easily absorbed by the other so are difficult to untangle even now.

Many critics consider his mastery of vocabulary, rhyme and metre impressive, although he has also been criticised for his florid style and word choices that only fit the rhyme scheme rather than contributing to the meaning of the piece. A. E. Housman, although a critic, had great praise for his rhyming ability: to Swinburne the sonnet was child's play: the task of providing four rhymes was not hard enough, and he wrote long poems in which each stanza required eight or ten rhymes, and wrote them so that he never seemed to be saying anything for the rhyme's sake.

Throughout his career Swinburne published literary criticism of great worth. His deep knowledge of world literatures contributed to a critical style rich in quotation, allusion, and comparison. He is particularly noted for discerning studies of Elizabethan dramatists and of many English and French poets and novelists. As well he was a noted essayist and wrote two novels.

Swinburne was nominated for the Nobel Prize in Literature every year from 1903 to 1907 and then again in 1909.

H.P. Lovecraft, the master of the dark side and a decent poet himself, considered Swinburne "the only real poet in either England or America after the death of Mr. Edgar Allan Poe."

Swinburne was also responsible for devising a poetic form called the roundel, a variation of the French Rondeau form.   In 1883 he published A Century of Roundels with several of the roundels dedicated to Dante's sister, the poet Christina Georgina Rossetti. Swinburne wrote to Edward Burne-Jones in 1883: "I have got a tiny new book of songs or songlets, in one form and all manner of metres ... just coming out, of which Miss Rossetti has accepted the dedication. I hope you and Georgie [his wife Georgiana] will find something to like among a hundred poems of nine lines each, twenty-four of which are about babies or small children".

Opinions of the Roundel poems move between those who find them captivating and brilliant, to others who find them merely clever and contrived. One of them, A Baby's Death, was set to music by the English composer Sir Edward Elgar as the song "Roundel: The little eyes that never knew Light".

After the first Poems and Ballads, Swinburne's later poetry was devoted more to philosophy and politics, including the unification of Italy, particularly in the volume Songs before Sunrise. He did not stop writing love poetry entirely, indeed it was only in 1882 that his great epic-length poem, Tristram of Lyonesse, was published, its contents lyrical rather than shocking. His versification, and especially his rhyming technique, remain of high quality to the end.

Algernon Charles Swinburne died of influenza, at the Pines in London on April 10th, 1909 at the age of 72.   He was buried at St. Boniface Church, Bonchurch on the Isle of Wight.

Algernon Charles Swinburne – A Concise Bibliography

Verse Drama

The Queen Mother (1860)
Rosamond (1860)
Chastelard (1865)
Bothwell (1874)
Mary Stuart (1881)
Marino Faliero (1885)
Locrine (1887)
The Sisters (1892)
Rosamund, Queen of the Lombards (1899)

Poetry
Atalanta in Calydon (1865)*
Poems and Ballads (1866)
Songs Before Sunrise (1871)
Songs of Two Nations (1875)
Erechtheus (1876)*
Poems and Ballads, Second Series (1878)
Songs of the Springtides (1880)
Studies in Song (1880)
The Heptalogia, or the Seven against Sense. A Cap with Seven Bells (1880)
Tristram of Lyonesse (1882)
A Dark Month & Other Poems
A Century of Roundels (1883)
A Midsummer Holiday and Other Poems (1884)
Poems and Ballads, Third Series (1889)
Astrophel and Other Poems (1894)
The Tale of Balen (1896)
A Channel Passage and Other Poems (1904)

*Although formally tragedies, Atlanta in Calydon and Erechtheus are traditionally included with his poetry.

Criticism
William Blake: A Critical Essay (1868, new edition 1906)
Under the Microscope (1872)
George Chapman: A Critical Essay (1875)
Essays and Studies (1875)
A Note on Charlotte Brontë (1877)
A Study of Shakespeare (1880)
A Study of Victor Hugo (1886)
A Study of Ben Johnson (1889)
Studies in Prose and Poetry (1894)
The Age of Shakespeare (1908)
Shakespeare (1909)

Major Collections
The Poems of Algernon Charles Swinburne, 6 vols. 1904.
The Tragedies of Algernon Charles Swinburne, 5 vols. 1905.

The Complete Works of Algernon Charles Swinburne, 20 vols. Bonchurch Edition. 1925-7.
The Swinburne Letters, 6 vols. 1959-62.